LADDER LEADERS

The Team

The Task

The Transition

STUDY GUIDE

SAM CHAND

Copyright © 2021 by Sam Chand

Published by Inspire

All rights reserved. No portion of this book may be reproduced, stored in a retrieval system, or transmitted in any form or by any means—electronic, mechanical, photocopy, recording, scanning, or other—except for brief quotations in critical reviews or articles, without prior written permission of the author.

Scripture quotations marked KJV are taken from the King James Version of the Bible. Public domain. | Scripture quotations marked NIV are taken from the Holy Bible, New International Version®, NIV®. Copyright © 1973, 1978, 1984, 2011 by Biblica, Inc.™ Used by permission of Zondervan. All rights reserved worldwide. www.zondervan.com. The "NIV" and "New International Version" are trademarks registered in the United States Patent and Trademark Office by Biblica, Inc.™ | Scripture quotations marked NKJV are taken from the New King James Version®. Copyright © 1982 by Thomas Nelson. Used by permission. All rights reserved. | The ESV® Bible (The Holy Bible, English Standard Version®). ESV® Text Edition: 2016. Copyright © 2001 by Crossway, a publishing ministry of Good News Publishers. The ESV® text has been reproduced in cooperation with and by permission of Good News Publishers. Unauthorized reproduction of this publication is prohibited. All rights reserved. | Scripture quotations marked ASV are taken from the American Standard Version (ASV). This Bible is in the public domain. | Scripture quotations marked AMP are taken from the Amplified Bible (AMP) Copyright © 2015 by The Lockman Foundation, La Habra, CA 90631. All rights reserved. | Scripture quotations marked NLT are taken from the Holy Bible, New Living Translation, copyright © 1996, 2004, 2015 by Tyndale House Foundation. Used by permission of Tyndale House Publishers, Inc., Carol Stream, Illinois 60188. All rights reserved.

For foreign and subsidiary rights, contact the author.

Cover design by: Joe De Leon

ISBN: 978-1-954089-27-3   1 2 3 4 5 6 7 8 9 10

Printed in the United States of America

CONTENTS

PART 1. WHO'S HOLDING YOUR LADDER? 5
- Chapter 1. Discover 6
- Chapter 2. Develop 12
- Chapter 3. Deploy 18

PART 2. MASTERING THE RUNGS 25
- Chapter 4. Focus 26
- Chapter 5. Communication 32
- Chapter 6. Decision-Making 38
- Chapter 7. Change & Transition 44
- Chapter 8. Conflict 50
- Chapter 9. Alignment 56
- Chapter 10. Money 62
- Chapter 11. Delegation 68
- Chapter 12. Execution 74
- Chapter 13. Future Thinking 80

PART 3. THE TRANSITION 87
- Chapter 14. Discontent & Discernment 88
- Chapter 15. Values & Passion 94
- Chapter 16. Wise Counsel 100
- Chapter 17. Desires & Timing 104
- Chapter 18. Internal Transition 108
- Chapter 19. External Transition 112
- Chapter 20. The Ladder to Legacy 116

PART 1

WHO'S HOLDING YOUR LADDER?

chapter 1

DISCOVER

If the fulfillment of our vision is dependent not only on our own commitment and competence, but on that of the teams that we gather around us, could there be a more crucial task than discovering, developing and deploying those ladder holders? After all, they may determine the difference between our success and failure.

Reading Time

As you read Chapter 1: "Discover" in *Ladder Leaders*, review, reflect on, and respond to the text by answering the following questions.

Why are ladder holders crucial to an organization's success?

___

Can you identify common red flags when it comes to selecting ladder holders?

___

Reflect on

Matthew 20:26 (NIV)

But among you it must be different. Whoever wants to be a leader among you must be your servant.

Consider Matthew 20:26, and answer the following questions:

How can you begin to incorporate the idea of servanthood into leadership development?

_____
_____
_____
_____
_____
_____
_____
_____

How do you identify Jesus' penchant for service leadership?

_____
_____
_____
_____
_____
_____
_____

How would you encourage others to aspire to serve as they aspire to grow as leaders?

___

What are the potential pitfalls of working with such individuals?

Sam identifies five positive qualities to look for in ladder holders. Can you add any to this list? Why are those qualities important to you?

_____
_____
_____
_____
_____
_____

Sam states that "you hire people for what they know; you fire them for who they are." How might problems be mitigated if you were to allow the reasons you dismiss people to more heavily influence those you bring on board?

_____
_____
_____
_____
_____
_____
_____

Why are volunteers not always the best ones for the job?

_____
_____
_____
_____
_____
_____

For the sake of your organization's success, it is more imperative for you to adopt a CEO and make swift decisions to eliminate issues or a pastoral one to attempt to excuse, overlook, or otherwise delay getting rid of the problem? Is this a challenge for you? Why or why not?

_____
_____
_____
_____
_____
_____

What does it mean that it is better to have a vacancy than bad help?

_____
_____
_____
_____
_____
_____

Ultimately, why is a culture of recruits superior to one of volunteers?

_____
_____
_____
_____
_____
_____

chapter 2

DEVELOP

*Mentoring isn't about the big things;
it is about the small ones.*

Reading Time

As you read Chapter 2: "Develop" in *Ladder Leaders*, review, reflect on, and respond to the text by answering the following questions.

What is the primary difference between training and development?

_____
_____
_____
_____
_____
_____
_____
_____
_____
_____

Why should leaders have multiple people developing them?

_____
_____
_____
_____
_____
_____
_____
_____
_____
_____
_____

Reflect on

—Proverbs 27:17 (ESV)

Iron sharpens iron, and one man sharpens another.

Consider Proverbs 27:17, and answer the following questions:

What examples of biblical mentorship can you identify?

_____
_____
_____
_____
_____
_____
_____
_____

Why do you think God calls us to mentor one another?

_____
_____
_____
_____
_____
_____
_____
_____

How can you approach your mentoring behaviors in a godly, biblical way?

___

Consider the three key ingredients Sam lists as the raw material for leadership development. Why do you think these elements are critical? Do you agree that everyone is born a potential leader? Why or why not?

___

What mentoring styles have others used effectively to help you develop your own leadership skills?

Are you aware of your own inadequacies to the degree you can be cognizant to not pass them on?

Why do good leaders easily transition from company to company? How are their talents best demonstrated?

Have you fully and honestly assessed yourself internally? Are you in touch with your own emotional and psychological state to the degree necessary to address those in others?

What are ways to monitor progress in your constituents?

Sam suggests that when your people begin to mentor others, they are progressing. Have you observed this? Recall an instance when someone you have mentored began to mentor another.

Leadership is about being rather than doing; it is about who rather than what. Are your current leadership strategies and priorities in line with this? If not, how can you begin to make the shift?

chapter 3

DEPLOY

Every true disciple of Jesus Christ holds somebody's ladder. That's God's plan. We need each other, and we fulfill God's plan when we hold others' ladders.

Reading Time

Read Chapter 3: "Deploy" in *Ladder Leaders*, review, reflect on, and respond to the text by answering the following questions.

Why might the process of developing leaders be threatening at times?

_____
_____
_____
_____
_____
_____
_____
_____
_____
_____

Do you consider the equipping leaders as an exit or an expansion strategy? Why is it important to differentiate the two?

_____
_____
_____
_____
_____
_____
_____
_____
_____
_____

Reflect on

Numbers 18:24 (NLT)

I have given them the Israelites' tithes, which have been presented as sacred offerings to the Lord. This will be the Levites' share. That is why I said they would receive no allotment of land among the Israelites.

Consider Numbers 18:24, and answer the following questions:

The Lord instructed the Israelites to support the Levites so they could serve in the Tabernacle. How does this relate to ladder holding?

_____
_____
_____
_____
_____
_____
_____

What might be the motivation behind the instruction to lend such support?

_____
_____
_____
_____
_____
_____

How can you hold the ladders of others who come behind you?

Consider Sam's example of the second-chair fiddle player. How does this example help illuminate the challenges of leader development?

Why do you think "ladder holding" is only half of proper leader development? How does this translate to discipleship?

___

Do you consider yourself to be a ladder holder? For whom? What qualities make a good ladder holder?

___

How does the concept of tithing correlate to ladder holding?

___

In the section "From Climbers to Holders," Sam lists several questions. As you consider those, what revelations can you derive about yourself?

How can you be an intentional mentor?

What is the legacy of mentorship you are creating for those who come behind you?

PART 2

MASTERING THE RUNGS

chapter 1

FOCUS

If we look around at our growing organizations and see that the people are confused, before blaming them we need to stop and ask, "How focused am I?" When we get out of focus, our people are unsure how to respond and unable to move forward.

Reading Time

Read Chapter 4: "Focus" in *Ladder Leaders*, review, reflect on, and respond to the text by answering the following questions.

How difficult is it for you to find and maintain focus?

_____
_____
_____
_____
_____
_____
_____
_____
_____
_____

Sam makes the point that our calendars can easily become hijacked by the agendas of others. How can you take control of your daily schedule?

_____
_____
_____
_____
_____
_____
_____
_____
_____
_____

Reflect on

Proverbs 4:25 (ESV)

Let your eyes look directly forward, and your gaze be straight before you.

Consider Proverbs 4:25, and answer the following questions:

What role does focus play in good leadership?

___

What is your personal motivation for establishing and daily strengthening your focus?

___

How can you help others maintain their focus?

Consider the warning signs of distraction: getting marginalized, getting attacked, getting seduced. Which of these do you notice most prominently in your life? What are some ways you can avoid it?

How do you define focus? Is this definition consistent for you and your organization?

_____

_____

_____

_____

_____

_____

Sam suggests that leaders can do eight things simultaneously with positive outcomes. What role does multitasking play in your life and role? How adept do you expect others to be at multitasking? Are these reasonable expectations?

_____

_____

_____

_____

_____

_____

How can you help lead people to the right hats?

_____

_____

_____

_____

_____

_____

Why is it important that what we focus on emanates from who we are?

_____
_____
_____
_____
_____
_____
_____

What are the key points to consider when communicating priorities and areas of focus?

_____
_____
_____
_____
_____
_____
_____

Identify at least two ways you can streamline your focus and that of others.

1. _____
_____
_____
_____

2. _____
_____
_____
_____

chapter 5

COMMUNICATION

As leaders we can be both concrete and abstract; but our followers or employees may only think concretely. We can broadcast in both AM and FM, but they can only hear AM. We have to make sure we broadcast the vision in a way the receiver can hear it.

Reading Time

Read Chapter 5: "Communication," in *Ladder Leaders*, review, reflect on, and respond to the text by answering the following questions.

Do you consider yourself to be a concrete or abstract thinker? How does this impact your leadership style?

_____
_____
_____
_____
_____
_____
_____
_____
_____
_____
_____

What can you adjust to become a more concrete communicator?

_____
_____
_____
_____
_____
_____
_____
_____
_____
_____
_____
_____
_____

> **Reflect on**
>
> James 1:19 (NLT)
>
> *Understand this, my dear brothers and sisters: You must all be quick to listen, slow to speak, and slow to get angry.*

Consider James 1:19, and answer the following questions:

When are you tempted to speak before listening?

_____
_____
_____
_____
_____
_____
_____
_____

What are ways you can develop better listening skills?

_____
_____
_____
_____
_____
_____
_____
_____

How can you entrust your tongue to God?

Why is communicating only when you have needs a poor communication habit?

How would you grade your follow-up, response, and degree of courtesy in your current communication habits? Where do you see room for improvement?

_____
_____
_____
_____
_____
_____

What role does listening play in effective communication? How are your listening skills?

_____
_____
_____
_____
_____
_____

Sam lists three components of empathetic listening. With which of these do you most resonate? How can you plan on implementing them as part of your personal communication habits?

1. _____
2. _____
3. _____
_____
_____
_____
_____

Why is it your responsibility as a good leader to communicate effectively?

_____
_____
_____
_____
_____
_____
_____

What role does self-talk play in effective communication?

_____
_____
_____
_____
_____
_____
_____

What do you typically do when you engage a discussion? How can you become more aware of your weaknesses and areas of improvement regarding your communication style?

_____
_____
_____
_____
_____
_____

chapter 6

DECISION-MAKING

Decision-making is an art and a science.

Reading Time

Read Chapter 6: "Decision-Making," in *Ladder Leaders*, review, reflect on, and respond to the text by answering the following questions.

Do you consider yourself to be a situational or principled decision maker? What is the difference between the two?

_____
_____
_____
_____
_____
_____
_____
_____
_____
_____
_____

Why is consistency and security associated with principled decision making more so than with situational?

_____
_____
_____
_____
_____
_____
_____
_____
_____
_____
_____

Reflect on

Proverbs 16:9 (ESV)

The heart of man plans his way, but the Lord establishes his steps.

Consider Proverbs 16:9, and answer the following questions:

What do you think Solomon was trying to convey when he wrote this?

_____
_____
_____
_____
_____
_____
_____
_____
_____

How can you entrust your decision-making to God?

_____
_____
_____
_____
_____
_____
_____
_____

What are ways you can purposely seek to place God's directives above your own from day-to-day?

What are the four steps of decision-making, as laid out by Sam?

Do you currently, consciously or unconsciously, employ these steps? How can you become more aware of your decision making strategies? Why is this beneficial?

How can you turn the bad decisions of others into opportunities for growth?

Consider the four questions Sam articulates when making complicated decisions. Why do you think the order is important?

Think about a recent complicated decision you had to make. Did you incorporate these four questions? In retrospect, how might they have benefited or how did they benefit your decision-making process?

_____
_____
_____
_____
_____
_____
_____

Are you able to explain the rationale behind your most recent decisions? Why is this important?

_____
_____
_____
_____
_____
_____
_____

How can you practically incorporate better decision-making practices into your leadership style?

_____
_____
_____
_____
_____
_____

chapter 7

CHANGE & TRANSITION

It is rare that change itself causes problems; typically, the culprit is a lack of transitional planning.

Reading Time

Read Chapter 7: "Change & Transition," in *Ladder Leaders*, review, reflect on, and respond to the text by answering the following questions.

Articulate the difference between change and transition.

_____
_____
_____
_____
_____
_____
_____
_____
_____
_____

How can understanding the difference between the two make you a better leader?

_____
_____
_____
_____
_____
_____
_____
_____
_____
_____
_____

Reflect on

Isaiah 43:19 (NIV)

See I am doing a new thing! Now it springs up; do you not perceive it? I am making a way in the wilderness and streams in the wasteland.

Consider Isaiah 43:19, and answer the following questions.

How can you learn to embrace and anticipate the change God brings about?

___

How can you help others see God's hand in times of transition?

___

Have you experienced times of positive change? What made the experience good? How can you incorporate that into your current phase of life?

_____
_____
_____
_____
_____
_____
_____
_____
_____

Why, according to William Bridges, do most change agents fail? Can you recall a time when you focused more on the solution than the problem? What were the results?

_____
_____
_____
_____
_____
_____
_____
_____
_____

How can you be proactive in maneuvering the "inevitable bumps" that accompany transition?

Can you recall an instance of a change that occurred without a transition? How did you approach the situation?

Why is assimilating new people into leadership such a challenge?

Effective leader transition requires the development and execution of a transitional plan. What do you think are the primary components of such a strategy?

Consider your level of personal responsibility when it comes to successful transition and change. How can you keep yourself accountable to seeing these processes through?

chapter 8

CONFLICT

A lack of conflict doesn't signal progress, but it might signal inactivity. Conflict is something that will always be. It is neither good nor bad, it simply is.

Reading Time

Read Chapter 8: "Conflict," in *LadderLeaders*, review, reflect on, and respond to the text by answering the following questions.

What degree of conflict do you think currently exists within your organization? Is this a realistic perception?

_____
_____
_____
_____
_____
_____
_____
_____
_____
_____

Why might a lack of conflict indicate stagnation?

_____
_____
_____
_____
_____
_____
_____
_____
_____
_____
_____
_____

Reflect on

Ephesians 4:26 (ESV)

Be angry and do not sin; do not let the sun go down on your anger.

Consider Ephesians 4:26, and answer the following questions:

The Bible acknowledges that anger and conflict will occur. Does this make it easier for you to accept the existence of conflict within your organization?

_____
_____
_____
_____
_____
_____
_____
_____

What do you think it means to not let the sun set on your anger?

_____
_____
_____
_____
_____
_____
_____
_____

How can you help others deal with conflict and anger in a biblical manner?

What are potential benefits of conflict?

How do you identify unnecessary conflict and what are the strategies you would employ to mitigate it?

_____
_____
_____
_____
_____

Consider the phrase, "There will be blood on the floor." How does that statement make you feel? How does this relate to your degree of comfort with conflict and your approach to it?

_____
_____
_____
_____
_____
_____

What is the difference between "good" and "healthy" in terms of an organization, a relationship, or conflict? Why is it more important to aim for a "healthy" resolution of conflict rather than an agreement or disagreement?

_____
_____
_____
_____
_____

Why is it necessary to deal with the "what" rather than the "who" when it comes to conflict?

_____
_____
_____
_____
_____

How does the setting of a discussion about conflict impact the success of the conversation?

_____
_____
_____
_____
_____
_____

Sam recommends that as leaders, we should be able to look into the mirror and know that we did everything possible to resolve a conflict. Consider a recent situation in which you had to address a situation. Are you pleased with your effort? How can you improve moving forward?

_____
_____
_____
_____
_____
_____

chapter 9

ALIGNMENT

When a leader's vision and values are aligned with the organization's goals, the alignment will be reflected in everything they do.

Reading Time

Read Chapter 9: "Alignment," in *Ladder Leaders*, review, reflect on, and respond to the text by answering the following questions.

What role does alignment play in a functioning organization or church?

_____
_____
_____
_____
_____
_____
_____
_____
_____
_____

Why is it not a viable plan for a leader to adjust his or her vision to that of an organization that has shifted its priorities?

_____
_____
_____
_____
_____
_____
_____
_____
_____
_____
_____

Reflect on

Proverbs 16:3 (NIV)

Commit to the Lord whatever you do and He will establish your plans.

Consider Proverbs 16:3 and answer the following questions:

How does God factor into your current method of strategic planning?

___

What does it mean to be aligned with God?

___

How can you lead others to be aligned with God's plan?

Describe organizational alignment in your own words. To what degree is your current vision in line with your organization's?

Consider the two examples Sam provides—that of the church in Atlanta and that of the business that focuses on customer service. What types of practical steps could you take to gauge your organization's alignment as Sam explained in these two instances?

_____
_____
_____
_____
_____
_____
_____
_____

What is the relationship between alignment and strategic planning?

_____
_____
_____
_____
_____
_____
_____
_____

Consider the eight elements of strategic planning that Sam proposes. Do you currently employ these? Why might these questions be so critical to successful planning and alignment?

_____
_____
_____

How can you ensure that decisions that are made are actually implemented?

Why is it more important to make changes to informal connections rather than formal structure when implementing strategies and working towards goals?

chapter 10

MONEY

There isn't room in today's business climate to "fake it until you make it."

Reading Time

Read Chapter 10: "Money," in *LadderLeaders*, review, reflect on, and respond to the text by answering the following questions.

Reflect on the quote by P.T. Barnum, "Money is a terrible master but an excellent servant." How does this apply to you and your leadership role?

_____
_____
_____
_____
_____
_____
_____
_____
_____
_____

Are you satisfied with your current business acumen? What could you do to fill in the gaps in your personal knowledge or understanding of the financial savvy necessary for a successful organization?

_____
_____
_____
_____
_____
_____
_____
_____
_____
_____

Reflect on

Luke 14:28-30 (ESV)

For which of you, desiring to build a tower, does not first sit down and count the cost, whether he has enough to complete it? Otherwise, when he has laid a foundation and is not able to finish, all who see it begin to mock him, saying, 'This man began to build and was not able to finish.'

Consider Luke 14:28-30, and answer the following questions:

Why do you think the Bible encourages savvy money practices?

_____
_____
_____
_____
_____
_____
_____
_____

What are the potential consequences of poor financial planning?

_____
_____
_____
_____
_____
_____
_____

How can you ensure that your financial practices are aligned with God's directive?

Have you experienced a situation in which your lack of knowledge, or that of another's, regarding finances negatively impacted an organization you were leading or of which you were a part? What can you learn from this experience?

Are you readily able to ask for help when you need it? Why is this critical for a good leader?

_____
_____
_____
_____
_____
_____

What insecurities or areas of growth are you willing to acknowledge for the overall growth and success of your organization?

_____
_____
_____
_____
_____
_____

Why is it important to seek various sources of advice and help?

_____
_____
_____
_____
_____
_____

Have you ever balked at seeking financial help because of the expense? What was the outcome? What lessons did you learn?

___

Consider the four items Sam suggests that a good financial advisor give. Why are all four important and why might the order in which you receive each piece impact your organization?

___

Why must you never delegate vision and ultimate decision-making? How can you practically ensure that you "do what you do best"?

___

chapter 11

DELEGATION

The truth is, people are willing to help us; we just have to be willing to go through the pain of delegating.

Reading Time

Read Chapter 11: "Delegation," in *Ladder Leaders*, review, reflect on, and respond to the text by answering the following questions.

Recall a time when you had to decide to either take on a project or delegate it. What was your decision and how did it play out?

_____
_____
_____
_____
_____
_____
_____
_____
_____
_____

Do you find delegation difficult? Why or why not?

_____
_____
_____
_____
_____
_____
_____
_____
_____
_____
_____
_____

Reflect on

Matthew 10:16 (NIV)

I am sending you out like sheep among wolves. Therefore be as shrewd as snakes and as innocent as doves.

Consider Matthew 10:16, and answer the following questions:

In this verse, Jesus is sending His disciples out into the world to teach and heal and proclaim His message. What can you learn about delegation from Jesus' interaction with His disciples?

_____
_____
_____
_____
_____
_____
_____
_____

How did Jesus equip the twelve before sending them out? Was there a degree of risk in this mission?

_____
_____
_____
_____
_____
_____
_____

How can you apply Jesus' example to your personal process of delegation?

What prices have you paid due to non-delegation?

Delegation is often a control issue. How does this manifest in your life and what are some ways you can begin to relinquish control?

What are the things that inhibit you from delegating?

What is your pain threshold? What are you willing to do to expand it?

What is the antidote to pain, as described by Sam?

Of the three Ds, which comes most naturally to you? How can you become more comfortable with the others?

chapter 12

EXECUTION

If leadership is about anything, it is about managing expectations. Our job is to minimize the distance between expectations and reality.

Reading Time

Read Chapter 12: "Execution," in *Ladder Leaders*, review, reflect on, and respond to the text by answering the following questions.

Do you relate to the story of the pastor that Sam tells at the beginning of the chapter? Describe your own similar experience.

_____
_____
_____
_____
_____
_____
_____
_____
_____
_____

Why is leadership about managing expectations? Have you found this to be true in your own leadership experience?

_____
_____
_____
_____
_____
_____
_____
_____
_____
_____
_____
_____

Reflect on

Proverbs 16:23 (ESV)

The heart of the wise makes his speech judicious and adds persuasiveness to his lips.

Consider Proverbs 16:23, and answer the following questions:

As a leader, why is your speech and communication so critical to successful execution?

_____
_____
_____
_____
_____
_____
_____
_____
_____

How can you rely upon God to guide your tongue?

_____
_____
_____
_____
_____
_____
_____

What are daily practices in which you can engage to ensure that your communication is clear, concrete, and in line with God's directive for your life and organization?

What is the question that must be answered in a meeting before moving from one agenda item to another? What happens if this is not accomplished?

What is the importance of specificity when referring to time?

_____
_____
_____
_____
_____
_____
_____

Consider the quote by John Maxwell, "People don't do what you expect; people do what you inspect." How does this resonate with you?

_____
_____
_____
_____
_____
_____
_____
_____

What practical steps can you take to see results and avoid conflict?

_____
_____
_____
_____
_____
_____
_____

chapter 13

FUTURE THINKING

Leaders need to spend less time looking at the past and more time anticipating the future.

Reading Time

Read Chapter 13: "Future Thinking," in *Ladder Leaders*, review, reflect on, and respond to the text by answering the following questions.

Why is it important to spend less time ruminating on the past and more time anticipating what is to come?

_____
_____
_____
_____
_____
_____
_____
_____
_____
_____

How well did your training equip you for today's multimedia demands?

_____
_____
_____
_____
_____
_____
_____
_____
_____
_____
_____

Reflect on

Romans 8:18 (ESV)

For I consider that the sufferings of this present time are not worth comparing with the glory that is to be revealed to us.

Consider Romans 8:18, and answer the following questions:

What wisdom do you see in these verses?

_____

_____

_____

_____

_____

_____

_____

_____

How do you think God wants you to think of the future?

_____

_____

_____

_____

_____

_____

_____

_____

Are you able to set aside current or past discomfort or pain and trust in the hope of a better tomorrow?

How did the events of 2020 impact your perception of the future?

Who would you consider to be a futuring leader? What makes them so?

_____
_____
_____
_____
_____
_____
_____
_____
_____
_____

How does your vocabulary factor into the type of leader that you are? What adjustments do you need to make to ensure that you are a futuring leader?

_____
_____
_____
_____
_____
_____
_____
_____
_____
_____

Why is it important to make sure your teammates are also future gazers and planners?

_____
_____
_____
_____
_____
_____
_____
_____
_____
_____
_____

Sam states, "The leaders who got us to this point may not be the ones who carry us into the future." How does this strike you? If this is a difficult lesson to learn, consider why and contemplate the implications of new leadership within your organization.

_____
_____
_____
_____
_____
_____
_____
_____
_____
_____
_____

PART 3

THE TRANSITION

chapter 11

DISCONTENT & DISCERNMENT

That's when I understood the concept of godly discontent. It meant I was all right, and no matter how much effort I forced, I would grow even more disenchanted.

Reading Time

Read Chapter 14: "Discontent & Discernment," in *Ladder Leaders*, review, reflect on, and respond to the text by answering the following questions.

Have you experienced godly discontent? Recall the situation. How did it impact you?

What does "more" mean to you?

Reflect on

1 John 4:1 (ESV)

Beloved, do not believe every spirit, but test the spirits to see whether they are from God, for many false prophet have gone out into the world.

Consider 1 John 4:1, and answer the following questions:

What role does discernment play in leadership and transition?

_____
_____
_____
_____
_____
_____
_____
_____
_____

How can you guard against false prophets or false leadings?

_____
_____
_____
_____
_____
_____
_____
_____

What does it mean to test the spirits? How might you do that?

___

Are you cognizant of your inner groanings? What do they say to you?

Have you been or are you in a position in which you were/are ready to switch ladders? Do you know which ladder you will reach for next? Does it seem riskier to stay where you are or look for what's next?

How can you discern whether the discontent you are experiencing is coming from God?

Contemplate the question Sam poses: *Do I know how God speaks to me?* Why is this a critical matter?

_____
_____
_____
_____
_____
_____
_____

Consider the four ways Tim Elmore suggests that God speaks to us. How have you experienced these?

_____
_____
_____
_____
_____
_____
_____

How can you live on the edge today?

_____
_____
_____
_____
_____
_____

chapter 15

VALUES & PASSION

I saw that my value was as simple as the words of Jesus. He said that the first command was to love God totally and the second "is like it," that is, it is of equal importance: "Love your neighbor as yourself" (Matthew 22:39).

Reading Time

Read Chapter 15: "Values & Passion," in *Ladder Leaders*, review, reflect on, and respond to the text by answering the following questions.

How do you distinguish between a core value and an important concern?

_____
_____
_____
_____
_____
_____
_____
_____
_____
_____

How comfortable are you with probing deeply to discover your core values?

_____
_____
_____
_____
_____
_____
_____
_____
_____
_____

Reflect on

Matthew 22:39 (NIV)

"Love your neighbor as yourself."

Consider Matthew 22:39, and answer the following questions:

What shapes your core values?

_____
_____
_____
_____
_____
_____
_____
_____

What do you believe God has called you to do and to be?

_____
_____
_____
_____
_____
_____
_____
_____

How can you develop practices to strengthen your awareness of your core values?

Can you identify your three to five core values? If so, record them here. If you are unsure, consider the questions Sam poses. *What do you value most? What do you dream about?* Record your answers here.

What is your reaction to the questions, "Who am I?" and "What is my life purpose?" Have you ever taken the time to answer them? Consider the five questions Sam poses. Do you have answers for them?

_____

_____

_____

_____

_____

_____

_____

_____

_____

_____

_____

When do you feel the most effective in your life?

_____

_____

_____

_____

_____

_____

_____

_____

_____

_____

Sam presents this question that leaders should ask when moving from one position to another: *Am I passionate enough right now that I can envision staying at this job for the rest of my professional life?* How would you answer that about your current position?

How can you avoid the pitfalls of self-delusion?

chapter 16

WISE COUNSEL

Unless we open up and benefit from the wisdom of others, we're apt to make unwise decisions.

Reading Time

Read Chapter 16: "Wise Counsel," in *Ladder Leaders*, review, reflect on, and respond to the text by answering the following questions.

Do you regularly seek counsel from others? Why is this important?

_____
_____
_____
_____
_____
_____
_____
_____

How have your insecurities impeded you from seeking the wisdom of others? What were the repercussions?

_____
_____
_____
_____
_____
_____
_____
_____
_____
_____
_____
_____

> ## Reflect on
>
> Proverbs 11:14, (NKJV)
>
> *"Where there is no counsel, the people fail; but in the multitude of counselors, there is safety."*

Consider Proverbs 11:14, and answer the following questions:

Why do you think the Bible endorses the practice of seeking counsel?

_____

_____

_____

_____

What are the potential consequences of not seeking wisdom from others?

_____

_____

_____

_____

How can you be diligent in humbling yourself daily to the advice of others?

_____

_____

_____

_____

How can you ensure you are speaking to the correct people?

Create a profile of those from whom you would seek counsel.

Create a list of 12-15 people from whom you would seek advice and a game plan for connecting with each one.

What is the value of perspective to you?

chapter 17

DESIRES & TIMING

Although I had identified my passion for helping other leaders release their dreams, and I was confident that it was God's will for me to move forward in pursuing this transition, I still faced big questions that would help me determine how I would make the transition and what the new ladder would be that would take me to my new destination.

Reading Time

Read Chapter 17: "Desires & Timing," in *LadderLeaders*, review, reflect on, and respond to the text by answering the following questions.

Sam articulates four things that helped him make his decision. If you are contemplating a transition, what big questions do you need to answer before making the leap?

_____
_____
_____
_____
_____
_____
_____
_____
_____
_____

What role do control, freedom, and structure play in your life? How do these factors shape where you are and what you are doing?

_____
_____
_____
_____
_____
_____
_____
_____
_____
_____
_____

Reflect on

Ecclesiastes 3:1 (ASV)

"For everything there is a season, and a time for every purpose under heaven."

Consider Ecclesiastes 3:1, and answer the following questions:

Do you trust that God has perfect timing for you and your every step?

How can you practice patience as you see each season of your life through?

How does timing impact your decision making?

Can you think of an instance where a leader has stayed too long in his or her role? What can you learn from that situation?

Consider the DOCTOR acronym Sam shares. How could this be applicable to you and your decision making?

Sam mentions that he has a fact budget and a faith budget. How different do you think God's numbers and plans are from your own? How can you begin to think on two levels?

What is the role of your partner's support in your current roles and decision-making? How does this dynamic impact you?

chapter 18

INTERNAL TRANSITION

Once we know where we want to go, we can face the challenge. We can take action.

Reading Time

Read Chapter 18: "Internal Transition," in *Ladder Leaders*, review, reflect on, and respond to the text by answering the following questions.

What are the five stages of internal transition?

1. _____

2. _____

3. _____

4. _____

5. _____

How would you explain the notion of pre-contemplation to someone else?

_____
_____
_____
_____
_____
_____
_____
_____
_____
_____
_____
_____

> **Reflect on**
>
> Jeremiah 29:11 (ESV)
>
> *"For I know the plans I have for you, declares the Lord, plans for welfare and not for evil, to give you a future and a hope."*

Consider Jeremiah 29:11, and answer the following questions:

Are you willing to entrust your future plans to the Lord?

_____

_____

_____

_____

How can you see God moving in each stage of transition?

_____

_____

_____

_____

What are ways you can entrust God with your darkness, doubts, and each step of uncertainty on a daily basis?

_____

_____

_____

_____

The stage of contemplation addresses things that you know to be true. Write down at least three things that you know are true.

1. _____

2. _____

3. _____

Why do you think the darkness is a necessary stage of internal transition?

_____
_____
_____
_____

How have you experienced insight?

_____
_____
_____
_____

What is necessary to arrive at the point of action?

_____
_____
_____
_____

chapter 19

EXTERNAL TRANSITION

Our exit strategy is more important than our entrance. That is, how we leave is more important than how we came in.

Reading Time

Read Chapter 19: "External Transition," in *Ladder Leaders*, review, reflect on, and respond to the text by answering the following questions.

Why is it so critical to leave well?

_____
_____
_____
_____
_____
_____

Have you observed someone who took parting shots or spoke poorly of their previous organization after making a transition? What can you learn from these negative behaviors?

_____
_____
_____
_____
_____
_____
_____

What are some important elements to include and omit in a letter of resignation?

_____
_____
_____
_____
_____
_____
_____

Reflect on

Ecclesiastes 7:8 (ESV)

Better is the end of a thing than its beginning, and the patient in spirit is better than the proud in spirit.

Consider Ecclesiastes 7:8 and answer the following questions:

Why is the end of something so special?

_____
_____
_____

How can you strive for patience rather than pride during periods of transition?

_____
_____
_____
_____

Sam states that how you leave is far more important than how you came in. Given this, what are practical things you could do to ensure a smooth exit?

_____
_____
_____
_____

How do you want to be remembered?

If you were to exit your organization, how big of an issue would the relinquishment of control be for you?

Good leaders plan for their succession early. How might one go about doing this?

How could you avoid being a lame duck?

chapter 20

THE LADDER TO LEGACY

We must strive to finish well and finish strong, as our departures will shape how we are remembered and may even atone for some of the mistakes we will inevitably make in the course of our time as leaders.

Reading Time

Read Chapter 20: "The Ladder to Legacy," in *Ladder Leaders*, review, reflect on, and respond to the text by answering the following questions.

The first three months are a critical time for any transition. Why are these 90 days so critical to the success of a transition?

_____
_____
_____
_____
_____
_____
_____
_____
_____
_____

Consider the ten suggestions presented by Michael Watkins to help navigate transition. Of these, which comes most natural to you? Which would be more of a challenge and how would you go about meeting it?

_____
_____
_____
_____
_____
_____
_____
_____
_____
_____

Reflect on

Psalm 37:18 (AMP)

The Lord knows the days of the upright and blameless, and their heritage will abide forever.

Consider Psalm 37:18, and answer the following questions:

Why do you think the Bible encourages us to consider the heritage or legacy we will leave behind?

_____
_____
_____
_____

How does the Lord's knowledge of our internal and external being impact your perception of yourself?

_____
_____
_____
_____
_____

How can you be cognizant of this in your daily life?

_____
_____
_____
_____

When you think about the legacy you are leaving, think of an example of someone who left well; whose departure you not only admired, but would like to assimilate in some way. What made this transition so remarkable?

_____
_____
_____
_____
_____
_____
_____

Consider the small church that posted a list of the accomplishments of the former pastors. If such a list were to be made about you, how do you feel about the legacy you are creating?

_____
_____
_____
_____
_____
_____
_____

How prepared are you to relinquish your professional identity?

_____
_____
_____
_____
_____
_____

How would you answer this question: Am I significant to people because of who I am or what I do?

If you were to depart your organization, would it be able to sustain what you began? How can you ensure that it does?

Why is it critical to understand what you're leaving behind before you move forward?

www.ingramcontent.com/pod-product-compliance
Lightning Source LLC
Chambersburg PA
CBHW070203100426
42743CB00013B/3027